Astonishing Bats!

Astonishing Bats!

Paperback ISBN: 978-1-952924-07-1

Dedication

This book is dedicated to all children who have a love of nature and the world around them.

Acknowledgment

I gratefully acknowledge the loving support of my husband and family without whose encouragement this book would not have been possible. And to all my good friends who willingly give me helpful feedback, please know that you are more important to me than you realize. Lastly to the little brown bats found at Chautauqua, NY, who filled the night skies, dove in front of me while chasing bugs and provided countless moments of entertainment as my big sisters tried to evict them from our house on several occasions!

Do you think bats are scary? Lots of people do. That's too bad. Bats do not want to harm us.

Bats are astonishing!

Bats are mammals. Just like you,
me, cats and dogs.

Bats are the only mammals that can fly.
Did you know that bats fly better than birds?

There are big bats, tiny bats, cute bats
and very ugly bats.

I am called a flying fox bat. I am big and very cute! I love fruit.

I am called a bumble bee bat because I am so tiny. I am only 1.3 inches long.

I am a Maclaud's horseshoe bat. Some people think I amy ugly. I think I am handsome! The weird stuff on my face just helps me to find bugs.

There are over 1,200 different kinds of bats.
That is astonishing!

What do bats look like?

Bats are a lot like us.
Like all mammals,
bats have hair and are warm-blooded.

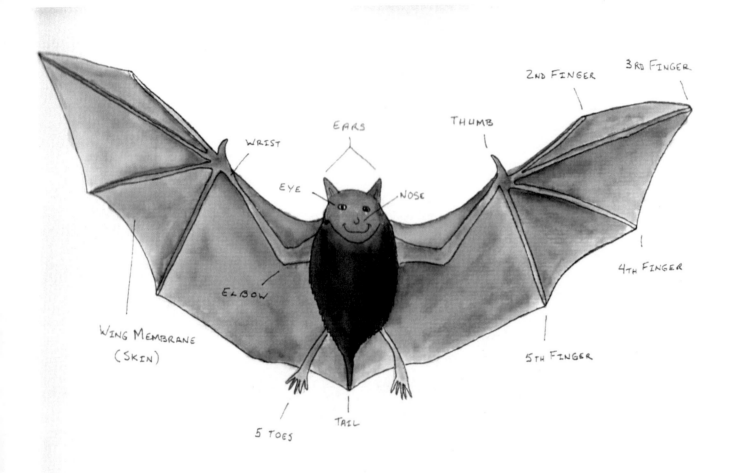

Bats have arms, legs, feet, hands and
many of the same bones we have.
Of course, they are much smaller.

Unlike us, bats have very long fingers.

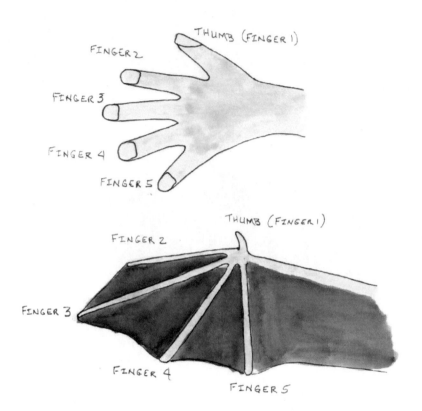

A bat's thin skin stretches over their legs, arms and fingers to form their wings.

Bats have furry bodies.

"Panda Bat" from South Sudan

Honduran White Bat

Little Brown Bat

Western Red Bat

Most bats are brown and black,
but some are colorful shades of orange or red.

Have you ever heard the expression
"blind as a bat"?

That is so not true! Bats can see very well.

Where do bats live?

Bats live nearly everywhere, except on a few islands and in the Antarctic.

I don't blame them!

Bats live in woods, deserts, towns and cities.
Their homes are called roosts.

Bats roost in places such as caves, trees and buildings, including house attics. They always try to find a place where they will be safe.

Bats also like to be near water
such as lakes, streams and ponds.

Bats can even swim! In fact, when they
have to, bats swim quite well.

What do bats eat?

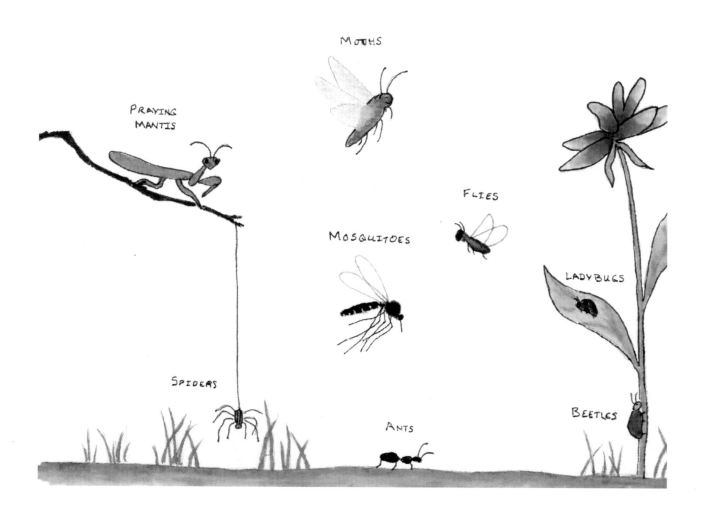

Most bats eat insects. Insect eaters are called insectivores.
I hope you are not an insectivore.

Bats use echolocation to catch bugs. Echolocation is when a bat makes a sound that will go out and bounce off objects right back to the bat.

That is how the bat knows exactly where that little bug is. Cool, right?

A bat can eat more than 600 bugs in one hour.
That is astonishing!

Some bats eat fruit. They are called frugivores.
That's a cool word.

Some bats do feed on blood.
These are called vampire bats.
They live in Central and South America.

These bats will make a small bite and lick the blood of large mammals, like cows. Some feed on birds. They do not try to hurt these animals and only drink about two teaspoons of blood.

Do bats sleep?

Since bats hunt for their food at night,
they sleep during the day for up to five hours.

Animals that sleep during the day and are active at night are
called nocturnal. That's another cool word.

Did you know that bats sleep upside down?

That is okay for bats, but I would'nt
want to do that. Would you?

Where do bat babies come from?

Momma bats have their babies in the spring.

Momma bats will join together in large groups called colonies
when they are ready to have their babies.

Each momma has just one baby.
Baby bats are called pups.

Momma bats keep their babies very close
and lovingly care for them.

How long do bats live?

Hi, Grandpa!

Bats can live between 20 and 40 years.

How do bats benefit people?

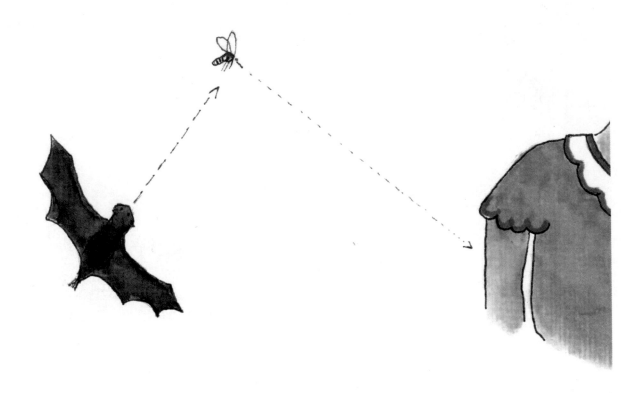

Bats eat mosquitoes and other bugs that carry disease and destroy food crops.

When bats in tropical rain forests poop, that poop, called guano, contains the seeds from the fruit they have eaten.

These seeds grow into trees. Nearly all new trees in the tropical rainforest come from the seeds dropped by bats

Now, don't you agree that
bats aren't scary?

Bats are astonishing!

Are you curious to know a little more about bats? Here are a few fun facts:

- Small woolly bats found in West Africa, live in large spider webs. Sticky!

- A vampire bat won't bite a person very often, BUT if it does, it will probably come back the next night to feed from that very same person. Why? Because vampire bats can tell people apart by the way they breathe. Ew!

- Some bats do not use their mouths to call out their ultrasound echolocation signals. Instead, they can use their nostrils.

- Bats first appeared 65 to 100 million years ago, which was the same time as the dinosaurs.

- Bat poop was used during the U.S. Civil War to make gunpowder.

- American author George W. Peck coined the phrase "bats in your belfry" in his 1899 book, Peck's Uncle Ike and the Red-Headed Boy.

- Al Kleberg used the term "batty" from his 1903 book, Slang Fables From Afar, when referring to one of his character. Apparently, she was a bit odd!

Source: Karin Lehnardt, "74 Interesting Bat Facts," Fact Retriever, updated September 5, 2019, www.factretriever.com/bat-facts.

Made in the USA
Monee, IL
15 December 2020